T0030409

Who Was Selena?

by Kate Bisantz and Max Bisantz

illustrated by Joseph J. M. Qiu

Penguin Workshop

To Selena's fans and the Quintanilla and Perez
families. Much love to AC, KB, DD—MB

To MB, SB, JB, JM, and RYR.
Also, the city of Lowell, MA, where my own Selena
fandom first began—KB

To Selena and all her fans—JQ

PENGUIN WORKSHOP
An imprint of Penguin Random House LLC, New York

First published in the United States of America by Penguin Workshop,
an imprint of Penguin Random House LLC, New York, 2018

Text copyright © 2018 by Kate Bisantz and Max Bisantz
Illustrations copyright © 2018 by Penguin Random House LLC

Visit us online at penguinrandomhouse.com.

Library of Congress Control Number: 2018022764

Printed in the United States of America

ISBN 9781101995495 (paperback)   12
ISBN 9781524786755 (library binding)   10 9 8 7 6 5

Contents

Who Was Selena?

On a hot day in 1993, tens of thousands of fans packed an outdoor arena in Monterrey, Mexico. The band onstage played its opening songs and the crowd began to push forward. They wanted to get closer to the person they came to see: a young singer from Texas who was known simply by her first name—Selena.

As the music played on, some fans shoved each other to get a better look. Others tried to climb onstage. The situation was getting dangerous.

Selena's father yelled from backstage to get out of there now! He didn't want the crowd to hurt his daughter. Selena and her band stopped playing and ran to the wings—the sides of the stage—for safety.

Once backstage, the band tried to find a way out of the arena. There was only one exit and the crowd was blocking it. Selena's father came up with a plan. He thought that if he spoke to the crowd, he could convince them to stop. He ran onstage and asked them to calm down. But this made the audience even louder. People started throwing cans and bottles. They were there to see Selena, not her father!

Selena understood their frustration. She told the band that she was going back onstage. She had just learned to speak Spanish and was determined to talk to the crowd herself. Everyone told her not to. They feared she could get hurt. But Selena never did what anyone expected. She trusted that her fans would listen to her.

Selena stepped back on the stage as the fans shoved and shouted. Smiling and calm, she spoke into the microphone, asking them to *cálmese, por favor.* Calm down, please.

Thousands of fans suddenly stopped pushing to listen to the twenty-two-year-old star. The band was amazed. One by one, they came back onstage and picked up their instruments. Then, Selena began to sing. Her voice filled the air and the crowd sang along to their favorite songs. The concert was a huge success.

Selena's understanding of her fans saved the show from disaster. It also helped her become the passionate musician that the world came to love.

CHAPTER 1
Texas Girl

Selena Quintanilla (say: KIN-tah-NEE-ya) was born on April 16, 1971, in Lake Jackson, Texas. It was a sunny and warm Friday in the spring. Her parents were Marcella and Abraham Jr., whom everyone called Abe. She had an older brother named Abraham III, or A.B. for short, and an older sister named Suzette. The Quintanilla

family was Mexican American. Their ancestors had immigrated to the United States from Mexico to search for work and a better future.

Life was hard in Texas for people with Mexican roots, or *Mexicanos* (say: MEH-hee-KAH-nohs). It had been that way for over a hundred years. Before the Mexican-American War began in 1846, South Texas had been a part of Mexico. People there were free to celebrate their heritage, which combined Aztec, Mayan, and Spanish cultures.

But in 1848, the United States took control of the land above the Rio Grande. Mexicans in Texas

Texas before 1848

now found themselves in American territory. White Americans, or *Anglos* (say: ANG-lohs), did not want them there. And Mexico itself was now divided. Southern Mexicans distanced themselves from Texas-Mexicans in the north, whom they called *Tejanos* (say: teh-HA-nohs), the Spanish word for Texan.

Even though they had been living on the land for generations, Tejanos faced a lot of prejudice. Abe had seen it himself as a boy in Texas. When he was in school, he was sent to the principal's office and hit for speaking Spanish. Some Anglos even put signs on their stores that read NO MEXICANS. And the city of Corpus Christi even went so far as to "code" their citizens by language and color.

Corpus Christi City Directory

Before the mid-1930s, the Corpus Christi, Texas, city directory listed each family by race and the language spoken at home. *C* stood for "Colored" (an outdated and offensive term for African American people), *M* stood for "Mexican," and *EM* stood for "English-speaking Mexican." Families with these letters by their names were often denied opportunities, like owning homes or having jobs, in their communities.

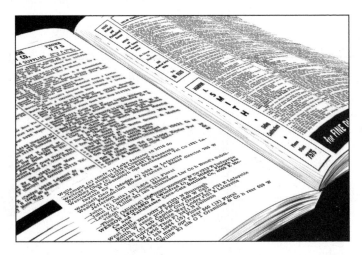

The directory was a public record, much like a phone book. Anyone could look up the codes. So, many Tejano parents stopped teaching their children Spanish. They thought it would give them a better life in America.

Corpus Christi stopped labeling families in this way by the 1940s. But the effects lasted for much longer. For many generations, Tejano children were taught to speak only English.

There were not many Mexicans in Lake Jackson. Marcella and Abe did not want their children to feel the unfair treatment that they had experienced growing up. It was important to them that Selena, Suzette, and A.B. fit in with their white neighbors and the Anglo children. Marcella and Abe taught their children to speak English instead of Spanish. Even Selena's name

was pronounced the Anglo way: "Seh-LEE-nah" instead of "Seh-LEH-nah."

Selena, Suzette, and A.B. loved growing up in Texas. The family had a home in a nice neighborhood and they had many friends. A flowering pink mimosa tree bloomed in their yard. Locals called the area "Snake Jackson" because it was so hot and green—it reminded them of the jungle.

The Quintanillas were Jehovah's Witnesses. This meant that the family spent many afternoons walking door-to-door preaching in their town.

Everyone loved Abe, Marcella, and their three well-behaved children.

Growing up, Selena was an adventurous tomboy. She played kickball outside and caught fireflies at night. She challenged boys to races

and usually won. If someone dared Selena to do something, she would do it. Though she was small, Selena was never one to back down from a challenge or a dare. One time at school, a friend dared Selena to flip her skirt over her head. Just as she did it, a teacher caught her in the act. Selena was completely embarrassed!

The teachers and students at O.M. Roberts Elementary School loved Selena. She was very polite, got good grades, and was always smiling. She even kept a good attitude when she had to skip other kids' birthday parties or holiday celebrations. Her religion didn't celebrate these things.

At home, Abe filled the days with music. It was important that his children share his passion. When Abe was young, he had been in a band called Los Dinos (say: lohs DEE-nohs). The band had been very successful in South Texas. But it wasn't successful *enough*. Abe had to leave the band behind to work in a factory, and sometimes drive a truck. He had to earn enough money to take care of his family.

Jehovah's Witnesses

Jehovah's Witnesses follow a branch of Christianity founded in the 1870s by a pastor named Charles Taze Russell in Pittsburgh, Pennsylvania. Russell's preaching created a movement called the International Bible Students Movement. Jehovah's Witnesses are the largest religious group to grow out of that movement.

Jehovah's Witnesses have a strong belief in Bible study and spreading the gospel to others. They often go door-to-door to preach. Most members do not celebrate birthdays, Christmas, Easter, and other holidays.

There are now over 8.3 million Jehovah's Witnesses around the world.

Teaching music was a way to pass his dreams down to his children. For Abe, it wasn't a hobby. It was required. When he taught A.B. to play the bass, they would practice for hours. Selena would get jealous and sing her father's favorite songs to get his attention. Her voice was strong and beautiful. Abe felt she was destined to become famous.

Abe saw that his children were talented enough to form a family band. A.B. played bass while Selena sang. Suzette played drums even though she hated them. She thought drums were for boys.

The band practiced almost every day in the garage. Abe taught the kids gospel and rock 'n' roll songs that he had known since his own childhood.

Selena, Suzette, and A.B. practiced more modern dance music that they heard on the radio.

The family played well together. Over time, the band became better and better. Abe signed them up to perform all over Texas. They played at small clubs and restaurants in Houston. They were the opening act for a band called La Mafia.

They even won two hundred dollars at a county fair!

Selena was still only eight years old and shy around strangers. But singing gave her confidence. Audiences couldn't believe such a beautiful voice came from someone so small. This little Texas girl was something special.

CHAPTER 2
Making Moves

In the summer of 1980, Abe decided to try something new. He started a restaurant called Papagayos, which means "parrots" in English. Once again, it was a family effort. Friends from church waited tables and Marcella took charge of the kitchen staff. They prepared a traditional Tex-Mex menu.

However, it soon became clear that Abe had much bigger plans than simply running a restaurant. He wanted to get back into show business. In

local papers, he advertised live entertainment at Papagayos. Local singers would perform for the customers during dinner service. But Selena and her siblings had top billing.

Sometimes Selena would sing while A.B. played bass and Suzette played the drums. Other nights, she would just be a regular kid and eat desserts in the restaurant kitchen.

One night, Primo Ledesma, a radio disc jockey, came into Papagayos when Selena was singing. He asked Abe if he could record his daughter. Abe agreed. The very next day, Selena's recording was played on the radio!

Specialties of the House

The combination of Mexican and American foods that are popular along the border of Texas and Mexico is known as *Tex-Mex*. Tex-Mex food is often confused with Mexican food, but it is cooked with different ingredients like pinto beans, yellow cheese, and ground beef.

- **Queso** (say: KAY-soh)—A melted cheese dip with chili added for spice. Often made with monterey jack or other processed cheese not found in Mexico.
- **Chili con carne** (say: CHEE-lee cohn CAR-nay)—A spicy stew of ground beef, chili peppers, tomatoes, and beans.
- **Burrito** (say: boo-REE-toe)—A flour tortilla wrapped around a filling that can include meat, beans, vegetables, cheese, or a combination of any of these.

Calls flooded in to the station asking about this young girl with the big voice. Someone even offered to pay her $2,000 to sing at a store opening in Houston—her first paying job!

Unfortunately, less than a year after it opened, Papagayos closed down. Abe had lost a lot of money. The family had to move in with one of Abe's brothers in a trailer park in El Campo, Texas.

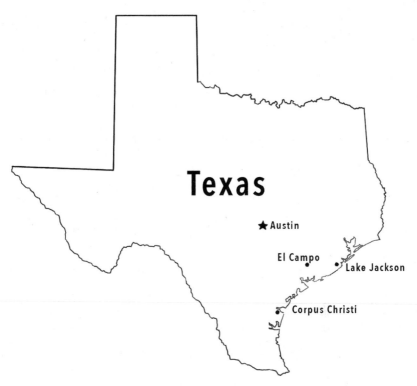

Texas

★ Austin

El Campo
•

• Lake Jackson

Corpus Christi

In El Campo, the family continued to work hard. Abe picked up odd jobs during the day, but he wanted his children to stay focused on their musical dreams. He felt that this was the time to get serious about making music their life's work.

The Quintanilla children's band officially became Selena y Los Dinos, named after Abe's original band. They began to play at weddings, anniversaries, and any event they could find. After a year, they had saved enough to move back to Lake Jackson.

Selena entered a local weekly talent show called *Star Mania*. And she won seven weeks in a row! In her small town of Lake Jackson, Texas, Selena felt like a star.

CHAPTER 3
For the Record

Selena y Los Dinos was good, but the band was only playing street fairs and weddings. They often played any song they thought would please the audience. Abe decided that the band should focus on only one type of music. They began learning to play Tejano music. People in Texas loved this music. Abe knew people would be happy to hear Selena sing in Spanish.

There were only two problems with Abe's new plan: Selena could barely speak Spanish, and she didn't even like songs that were sung in Spanish! She, A.B., and Suzette wanted to play the Top 40 hits they heard on the radio.

Abraham told them that Tejano may not be the music they loved, but it could make them famous. Night after night, he sat with Selena and taught her Spanish words and phrases so she could sing like a pro.

Abe knew it would be a struggle to make it big in Lake Jackson. For acting, everyone moved to New York City or Los Angeles. But for Tejano music, Corpus Christi, Texas, was the place to be. Many Tejano artists, like Freddy Fender and Laura Canales, lived and worked in Corpus Christi. It would take a lot of money to move the whole family, but Abe was convinced they should give it a try. To pay for the move, Abe sold the family boat and trailer. He packed up the van with instruments, amplifiers, and speakers and moved his family into his brother's house in Corpus Christi.

Tejano Music

Tejano is a term that describes the native music of Mexican Americans living in Texas. It has roots in traditional Mexican folk music, but also includes styles and sounds brought to Mexico by German, Polish, and Czech immigrants in the mid-1800s.

Traditional Tejano music is played by four musicians—known as a *conjunto*—on accordion, drums, bass, and a twelve-string guitar. It now includes the musical styles of many other cultures who call South Texas home. Some of the most popular are *ranchera*, *cumbia*, polka, and *corrido*.

For Selena, Corpus Christi was like a whole other world. It was too hot to play outside. And she missed the tall trees in Lake Jackson. She also missed her friends, and it wasn't easy getting used to a new school. But she knew the family was counting on her. And she loved performing with A.B. and Suzette. She began to get excited about what lay ahead—and even more determined to succeed.

When he felt they were ready, Abe took the band to meet Freddie Martinez. Freddie owned a record label in Corpus Christi called Freddie Records. It

Freddie Martinez

was here that the group recorded its first record in 1983. It was simply called *Selena y Los Dinos*.

The band began to play at weddings, anniversaries, fund-raisers, and anywhere Abe thought his children might get discovered.

However, it was hard being a young woman in a business with so many male stars. Not everyone thought Tejano music was a place for young girls. No matter how many doors shut in Abe's face, he kept trying to find opportunities for Selena and the band.

The Quintanilla family was spending a lot of time performing together. To pass the time backstage or in the van, the kids would play pranks on each other. Selena was the biggest prankster of them all. One of her favorite tricks was taking the cream out of Oreo cookies and replacing it with toothpaste. She also loved startling people by loudly imitating an opera singer hitting a high note.

Even though Selena y Los Dinos was earning money by playing as much as it could, the Quintanillas still struggled. Abe worked odd jobs during the day to support everyone. Eventually, they were able to move into their own house with a big backyard. The family finally had a real home in Corpus Christi.

Everything was starting to come together. In 1985, Selena y Los Dinos signed a new record deal with Cara Records. By this point, the band had grown to include other musicians as well, including Ricky Vela on keyboards and Roger

Garcia on guitar. Selena y Los Dinos released a cassette tape called *The New Girl in Town* that December. This Spanish-language album was an official introduction to the Tejano world.

One of the songs off the album, "Oh, Mama" started getting played on the radio. It also got the attention of a local TV host named Johnny

Canales. He invited Selena y Los Dinos to perform on his weekly music show called *The Johnny Canales Show*. At just thirteen,

Johnny Canales

Selena was about to be on television for the very first time.

The Quintanillas wanted to make sure viewers took her and the band seriously. She already had a grown-up voice, so they decided to give her a grown-up look. A short haircut made Selena appear a little older than she was. She, A.B.,

Suzette, and the rest of the band wore white jumpsuits they had decorated with neon paint and combat boots. Selena wore guitar-shaped earrings and joked with Johnny about her trouble speaking Spanish. People loved her.

But Selena's teachers were worried. Even though she was very smart, her career was interfering with her schoolwork. Teachers begged Abe and Marcella to stop letting Selena miss school all the time to perform.

But in the end, Selena's parents took her out of the eighth grade. They decided to homeschool her while the family performed. Shortly after she left school, Selena y Los Dinos signed with a new record label. Music was now their life.

CHAPTER 4
Entertainer of the Year

Now that she was being homeschooled, Selena's life revolved around her family and the band. Although she performed with A.B., Suzette, and the rest of the band as Selena y Los Dinos, Selena had quickly become the star. By the time she was fifteen, she had appeared alone on the cover of *Tejano Entertainer* magazine.

But Selena didn't have many friends her own age. Ricky Vela and Roger Garcia were older, and they were better friends with A.B. When she wasn't performing, she passed the time alone drawing pictures of new outfits and designing her own clothes. Music was something the Quintanilla family did together. Fashion was Selena's private passion.

Her siblings also had passions of their own. For her brother, that passion was songwriting. A.B. wanted to take Tejano music to the next level. He had written a song with Ricky called "Dame Un Beso" [say: DAH-meh OON BEH-soh], which means "give me a kiss." He used drum machines, a new idea in pop music at the time. It had never been done in Tejano music.

Suzette and Selena loved the song and were very proud of their brother. They let his new style influence their next album, *Alpha*.

By the summer of 1986, *Alpha* was being played everywhere. "Dame Un Beso" was very popular and became a hit song on the radio in Texas. Los Dinos officially had a new songwriter in the band: A.B.!

The next year, Selena's star power grew even more. She was nominated for Female Vocalist of the Year—not with the rest of Los Dinos—at the 1986 Tejano Music Awards. This was impressive for a girl so young, and shocking to many in the Tejano music world. But no one thought that a fifteen-year-old would beat the reigning queen of Tejano music, Laura Canales. When Selena was announced as the winner, it became front-page news.

After she was named the Female Vocalist of the Year, everyone wanted to hear more of Selena and her family band. Selena y Los Dinos released a new album called *And the Winner Is . . .* One of the songs on the album was a version of a traditional Mexican song called "La Bamba."

The song made its way into the Top 20 on the Billboard Latin chart. This means that Selena's song was the twentieth most popular Spanish-language song in the entire country!

In 1987, Selena was invited back to *The Johnny Canales Show* to perform "La Bamba." She had grown up a lot since the last time she was there. The sixteen-year-old singer wore a silver, sparkling bullfighter's outfit. She had big, teased hair, painted fingernails, and big hoop earrings.

Laura Canales (1954–2005)

Laura Canales was the most successful female Tejano singer of the 1980s.

Born in Kingsville, Texas, Laura began singing in high school. She found success in the Tejano music scene as a founding member of the group Felicidad, and later with her own band, Laura Canales & Encanto.

Laura Canales was known for songs like "Si Vivi Contigo" ("If I Lived with You") and "Dame La Mano" ("Give Me Your Hand"). During her career, she received the Yellow Rose of Texas award, along with Female Entertainer of the Year and Female Vocalist of the Year at the Tejano Music Awards.

In March of 1988, Selena won Female Entertainer of the Year at the Tejano Music Awards. It was time to officially take the act on the road. The family bought a tour bus they named Big Bertha. The outside of the bus was stylish and hip. But inside, it was a mess!

The bus had no heat or air-conditioning. Everyone slept on the floor. Still, the Quintanilla family kept their spirits high. Abe happily drove the family, the band, and all their equipment all over the big state of Texas.

That year, they performed in many towns, including San Antonio, Dallas, and Corpus Christi. Selena y Los Dinos sometimes performed two or more times a day in different cities. The band slept between shows or at roadside motels. When she had the time, Selena worked on her fashion designs.

During a trip to San Antonio, Selena went to see a Tejano singer named Shelly Lares perform. Behind her, she spotted a quiet, handsome guitarist with long hair. His name was Chris Perez.

Selena could tell that something about this talented musician was special. But she didn't have much time to think about him. She had too many shows to play and new songs to record. Even so, Selena's music and undeniable beauty had already caught Chris's attention.

Chris Perez was also very impressed with A.B.'s songwriting. He became friends with the band and was soon invited to start playing with them. Little by little, Chris and Selena grew closer. She was seventeen and he was nineteen. Neither one knew how a romance might affect the band. The only thing they were sure of was that Selena's career was on the rise.

CHAPTER 5
Young Love

In 1989, Selena was once again named Female Entertainer of the Year at the Tejano Music Awards. This time, no one was surprised. Everyone in the San Antonio Convention Center had come to see Selena.

Music executives wanted Selena to sign a contract with their record companies. It was clear that she was ready to become an international superstar. But who would be the one to expand the Tejano singer's career and popularity beyond Texas?

José Behar worked at a record company called Capitol/EMI Latin, which produced and promoted the music of Latin America, sung mainly in Spanish.

CAPITOL/EMI Latin

This includes a wide variety of styles such as salsa, samba, tango, bossa nova, and Tejano. José had a plan to turn Selena from a Texas Tejano singer into a world-famous star. The Quintanillas liked his plan and signed a recording contract with EMI Latin. But first, Selena would need a new look.

Selena was eighteen years old now. She didn't have to cut her hair short to look older. She was a beautiful young lady. And José wanted the world to see that on the cover of her new album, *Selena*. Though A.B. and Suzette would still play in her band, this was Selena's first solo album. She was now in her very own spotlight.

For the photo shoot, Selena chose a fashionable outfit with a flowing sheer skirt and a small, fitted top. Although in style at the time, it was surprising  for Selena to show off her bare stomach on the album cover. Marcella warned Selena that her father wouldn't like it very much. But Selena felt confident and pretty.

The fans agreed. The album had a hit song that reached number eight on the Hot Latin Tracks list in Mexico.

Her next album, *Ven Conmigo* [say: VEN cohn-MEE-goh], which means "come with me," did even better.

Selena's success caught the attention of the Coca-Cola Company. It had been looking for the perfect spokesperson to represent its soda brand in Latin America—the mostly Spanish-speaking countries south of the United States, including Mexico. Selena's cool teenage look paired with her Latin heritage made her the perfect face of the brand.

Selena signed a contract with Coca-Cola. For her first Coke commercial, the band wrote a tune that sounded just like a Selena song. Shortly after, they flew to Acapulco, Mexico, to celebrate.

The trip to Mexico was the first time Selena and Chris were able to be alone. Sitting together

on the plane, they began talking about their interests, their childhoods, and their dreams.

Suddenly, the plane hit some turbulence. Chris got scared and grabbed the armrest. Selena grabbed his hand. It felt natural. They talked for the rest of the plane ride, holding hands. When they landed in Texas, they both knew that something between them had changed.

Chris loved how lively and outgoing Selena was. Selena would often tease Chris about being so quiet. Their differences made them the perfect pair.

The two grew closer, but were careful to keep their romance a secret. Abe would not have approved. He wanted Selena's entire focus to be on her music.

Selena *was* committed to music, her family, and to Chris. But she also made sure to continue her education. In 1990, Selena's homeschooling paid off and she received her high-school diploma. She was proud of her accomplishment. Everyone could see that Selena was more than just a teenager with a beautiful voice.

Throughout all this excitement, Selena and Chris continued their romance in secret. One day, when the band was waiting for a show to start, the pair snuck off to get pizza. It was at a Pizza Hut in the Rio Grande Valley that the couple shared their first "I love you."

Traveling on a bus with the entire Quintanilla family made it even more difficult for Selena and Chris to hide their feelings. One by one, band members started to find out—even Marcella knew their secret. When Abe eventually did find out, he kicked Chris out of the band!

Selena was furious. She'd always done what her father had asked. This was the time for her to take a stand. She was an adult and she was in love. After weeks of pleading with Abe, she decided the only way she and Chris could be together was to get married. Now. No engagement, no announcement, no big wedding.

Chris and Selena were married on April 2, 1992. It was just the two of them at city hall. Selena didn't even wear a wedding dress. She didn't want her family to suspect anything when she left the house. But Selena and Chris were never happier.

They couldn't keep the marriage a secret, though. Selena was fast becoming a celebrity. The Quintanillas found out and called Selena. Her father couldn't deny the love that Selena and Chris shared. Abe finally accepted Chris into the family and back into the band. Selena was now officially married and had her entire family's love and support.

CHAPTER 6
Enter My World

Now that Selena and Chris were married, the Quintanillas could once again focus on their music. Selena was ready to take her act beyond Texas. She wanted to share her gifts with the whole world. And she was ready to sing in English. It was important to her that she express herself in her first language, too.

But turning a Tejano star into an English-language superstar would not be easy. José Behar wanted to make Selena known throughout Mexico and the rest of Latin America first. He believed that once she had enough Spanish-speaking fans, record companies would agree to let her make any kind of music she wanted.

The timing was perfect. Selena's new album,

Entre a Mi Mundo (say: en-TRAY ah mee MOON-doh), which means "enter my world," was already being played on Mexican radio. Fans in Mexico loved a song A.B. wrote called "Que Creías"—or "What Did You Think?" in English. Another hit off the album was called "Como La Flor" (say: KOH-MOH la FLOR), which means "like the flower." It was quickly a hit throughout Latin America and soon became one of her most popular songs.

José put together a Mexican tour. Selena was ready. But was Mexico ready to embrace an American woman who had only learned to speak Spanish over the last nine or ten years?

There was a lot of pressure for Selena to succeed. If the trip didn't go well, her whole family and band would have come all this way for nothing.

The first stop was Monterrey, Mexico. Local magazines, television crews, and newspaper reporters were waiting to meet Selena when she arrived. She hugged each and every reporter. She smiled and answered all their questions in the best Spanish she could. When she fumbled with a word, she made up for it by smiling and laughing.

Though she spoke a different language and was from another country, her warmth and generosity were universal.

All the reporters in Monterrey wrote glowing reviews of Selena. One newspaper called her an "artist of the people." Reporters loved her dark wavy hair and natural complexion. Most Mexican stars at the time dyed their hair blond and stayed out of the sun to look as Anglo as possible. But Selena was proud of her Mexican heritage. People felt a connection with the young singer.

After her success in Mexico, Selena came back to Texas with a new energy. She enrolled in Spanish classes to learn the language better. On February 7, 1993, she played to a packed arena back home in Corpus Christi. The concert was recorded and released as an album called *Selena Live!*

A few months later, Selena was back in Mexico and even more famous than before. She talked to

reporters with more confidence. She performed for thousands of Mexican fans. Tejano music acts had never been this successful in Mexico. When she returned to America, Selena performed for almost sixty thousand people at the Houston Livestock Show and Rodeo in the Astrodome. Selena-mania was taking hold.

But there was one burning question in Selena's life. Should she tell the world about her marriage to Chris? It had been hard enough for her own family to accept the couple. Would her fans? Many of Selena's fans were young men, or teenage girls who liked Selena's sassy, independent attitude.

But Selena was tired of secrets. And her fans deserved the truth. There had been rumors about Chris and Selena for months. It was time to set the record straight.

As a gift to Selena, Chris had his friend paint a picture of her face on his guitar. He started playing it onstage during the concerts. The crowd loved it. They were officially one of the biggest musical couples in the world.

At home, their life was just like any other newlywed couple. They moved into a house right next to Abe and Marcella and filled it with all their favorite things. One of those things was Pebbles,

Selena's dog. She loved animals, and Chris loved seeing her happy. This soon led to four more dogs, a python, and a giant fish-tank headboard for their bed!

It was nice to have a permanent home in Corpus Christi after so many years on the bus. She was able to spend more time with Chris and work with local charities. One of her favorites was a program dedicated to keeping kids in school. She knew how important an education was because she had had to work so hard to finish hers while traveling with the band.

Selena now had fans in Texas, Mexico, Spanish-speaking Latin America, and other parts of the United States. One fan, Yolanda Saldivar, approached the Quintanillas about starting an official Selena fan club. She wanted to help with fan mail,

Yolanda Saldivar

appearances, and merchandise. Suzette had been handling all of Selena's merchandise, but she could use a break. After all, she was also one of Los Dinos and had just gotten married!

Yolanda soon became the club's president. Selena and Yolanda became very close, and Yolanda was taken in as part of the family.

Yolanda called Selena *mija* (say: MEE-ha), which means "my daughter" in Spanish.

In November of 1993, Selena's biggest wish came true. Selena y Los Dinos signed an English-language record deal. Selena was on her way to becoming a superstar.

CHAPTER 7
Grammy Style

The Quintanilla family had sacrificed everything to succeed in the music industry. Now their dreams were coming true. For Abe, Selena's success proved that he had been right all along about her talent. For Marcella, it confirmed that raising her family on the road had been the right decision. Selena, A.B., Suzette, and Chris learned that all their hard work had been worth it. Their hit albums had reached the top of the Billboard music charts and sold millions of copies across the United States and Latin America.

Selena was proud of herself and her family. But now she wanted to do something for herself. She wanted to take her fashion ideas to the next level by starting her own clothing line. Since her

early days drawing pictures on the bus, designing clothes had always been her secret dream.

Selena had been making her own clothes and accessories for years. Sometimes she would buy a belt or jacket, cover it with rhinestones, and show off her sparkly creation onstage. Other times she would alter an entire outfit. Her style was becoming famous. Girls all over Latin America wanted to dress like Selena.

She had a small work
space in her house, but
there was no way she could
make enough clothes by
herself to create an entire
fashion line. A Texas
designer named Martin
Gomez stepped in to help

Martin Gomez

her. Martin used his degree in fashion design to
turn Selena's sketches into real clothes.

On January 27, 1994, Selena Etc. opened in
Corpus Christi. The shop featured all of Selena's
original clothing and accessories, plus a hair and
nail salon. Selena would often visit the store,

sometimes stopping by while wearing jeans and a T-shirt. Without her flashy stage outfits, no one recognized her. She loved watching customers try on her designs and leave Selena Etc. happy with their purchases.

Yolanda Saldivar became the manager of Selena Etc., in addition to running the fan club. And Martin Gomez stayed on to help with the fashions. Now that two people she trusted were looking after her store, Selena could go back to her music.

On March 1, 1994, Selena traveled with her family to New York City to attend the thirty-sixth annual Grammy Awards. *Selena Live!* had been nominated for Best Mexican-American Album. This was the first time Selena was nominated for a major international award. Everyone was very nervous.

Selena wore a white crystal beaded gown for the event at Radio City Music Hall in New York

City. She sat near the back of the auditorium with Chris, her family, and Los Dinos. They all held each other while waiting for the results.

"The Grammy goes to . . . ," the announcer said, ". . . *Live!* Selena."

Selena and her family jumped for joy. Selena walked quickly down to the stage, repeating one thought: *Don't fall!* She was worried she would trip over the hem of her dress!

Selena stepped onto the stage. She received her award and thanked Los Dinos, her family, and everyone at her record company.

"I love you," she said before she walked offstage.

A couple of weeks later, Selena won Female Vocalist of the Year, Female Entertainer of the Year, and Album of the Year at the Tejano Music Awards in San Antonio. That same month, she released her next album—*Amor Prohibido* (say: ah-MOR pro-ee-BEE-doh), which means "forbidden love."

One of the songs on the new album was called "Bidi Bidi Bom Bom." It was written almost by accident during rehearsal when Suzette, A.B., and Selena were goofing off.

A.B. started playing guitar, and Selena made up nonsense words on the spot. They all liked the sound of it, so they wrote real lyrics to complete the song.

Amor Prohibido become one of Selena's biggest albums. "Bidi Bidi Bom Bom" was a smash hit. The album went quadruple platinum—it sold more than four million copies! *Amor Prohibido* even knocked one of Selena's idols, Gloria Estefan, off the top of the Billboard Latin Tracks (Spanish-language) chart.

Gloria Estefan (1957–)

Gloria Estefan was born Gloria María Milagrosa Fajardo García in Havana, Cuba, during the Cuban Revolution. Shortly after her birth, her family moved to Miami, Florida. As a young woman, Gloria became the lead singer of a Cuban-inspired band called Miami Sound Machine. She married the band's leader, Emilio Estefan, in 1978. In 1985, Miami Sound Machine's song "Conga" became an international hit, and introduced the world to the modern Latin music that was being made in Miami called the "Miami Sound."

Gloria has won four Latin Grammy Awards, three Grammy Awards, an American Music Award of Merit, and a Presidential Medal of Freedom. Her powerful voice can be heard on songs like "Rhythm Is Gonna Get You," "Get on Your Feet," and "Oye." Gloria Estefan is often credited with making contemporary Cuban music a part of American pop culture.

In 2015, the Broadway musical *On Your Feet!* opened in New York. It is based on the life and music of Gloria and Emilio Estefan.

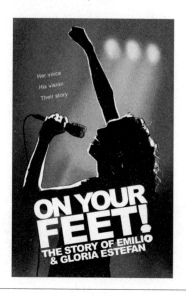

In September of 1994, a second Selena Etc. store opened in San Antonio, Texas. It seemed as if everyone wanted to dress like Selena. She still represented Coca-Cola in advertisements. But other companies now wanted Selena to sell their products, too. As her popularity grew, so did new business opportunities.

At Selena and Chris's house, there wasn't enough room to run a fashion line, practice music, have an office space, and live their lives. The Quintanilla family bought and remodeled an old building at 5410 Leopard Street in Corpus Christi.

The whole family moved their recording studio, clothing workroom, and offices into the new work space. Leopard Street was now the new home of Selena's Design House, Q Studios, and Q Productions.

CHAPTER 8
Dreaming of You

In late 1994, Selena prepared for a performance that made her more nervous than even her first shows at Papagayos had. She was going to San Antonio for her very own fashion show. Selena's clothes would be seen on the runway for both fans and fashion critics. This was the first time that Selena would be in the spotlight without her family, and for something other than her music.

Selena wore an ivory gown she'd made herself. She excitedly told reporters that if she hadn't gone into entertainment, she would have been a full-time fashion designer.

The fashion world loved her designs. Just like her music, she had something for everyone—glamorous pieces as well as modern, practical outfits.

Selena was eager to add other new businesses alongside her clothing line. She teamed up with Leonard Wong, who ran a cosmetics business, to create her own perfume. She told Leonard that she wanted to create something that was like her—strong, yet delicate. *Forever Selena* perfume was a mix of flowery, citrusy, and spicy scents.

Throughout all of this, Yolanda had been managing Selena's boutiques. But Martin Gomez was becoming concerned about Yolanda. He suspected that she had been stealing money and other items from the stores. He also didn't like how Yolanda seemed to control Selena. Some people couldn't even talk to Selena without getting Yolanda's permission first! In December of 1994, Martin told Abe about his concerns.

Abe tried to talk to Selena. She didn't believe

him. He had been wrong about Chris before they were married. Maybe he was wrong about Yolanda, too. She couldn't imagine that her friend would take money from the businesses.

Selena focused on the path ahead. She won Female Entertainer of the Year at the Tejano Music Awards once again. She also won Song of the Year for "Bidi Bidi Bom Bom." She was only twenty-three years old.

Selena's dreams of having a hit song in English became even more real in March of 1995. The family piled into Q Productions to listen to the first version of Selena's single: "Dreaming of You." The song—sung in English—was inspired by her love for Chris. You could hear the passion and feeling in her voice. This was the song that could change everything for her.

The Quintanillas knew it wouldn't be long before Selena became an international superstar. On March 11, 1995, she sang at a concert in Chicago. The family was thrilled to see such a diverse crowd—it was no longer just Tejano fans coming to hear Selena sing. All types of people, speaking both English and Spanish, were now Selena fans. The family's hard work was about to pay off. But there was one problem that needed to be taken care of.

More reports had come in about Yolanda's dishonesty. Selena could no longer ignore the issue. She, Abe, and Suzette confronted Yolanda. Suzette called Yolanda a liar and a thief. Selena and Abe told Yolanda she could not return to work.

Later, Selena realized that samples of her new perfume were missing. She wondered if Yolanda had taken them. And then Selena found out about something even worse: Yolanda had tried to take money out of Selena's bank accounts. Selena called Yolanda and demanded that she return the perfume samples and give her the bank records.

On March 31, 1995, Selena went to meet Yolanda in Corpus Christi. She wanted to get the information she needed, and then they would all be able to put the whole mess behind them. But Selena was very wrong about that.

When she arrived at the hotel where Yolanda was staying, Yolanda did not want to admit the truth. She thought she could make her problems go away by frightening Selena. But Yolanda did more than scare the young superstar. She shot Selena. Although she was rushed to the hospital, it was too late. At only twenty-three years old, the Queen of Tejano was gone.

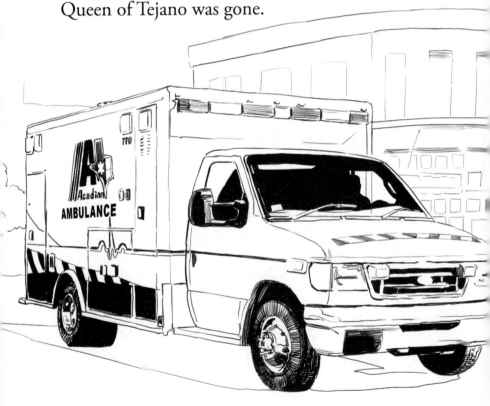

Television and radio stations broke the terrible news to listeners that very same day. Chris and the Quintanillas found out just as the rest of the world did. All of the music industry mourned, along with the fans and family she loved so much.

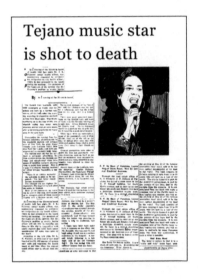

CHAPTER 9
Legacy

Thousands of fans gathered outside the two Selena Etc. stores and Q Studios on Leopard Street to leave flowers, candles, and cards. Candlelight vigils popped up around the world to honor Selena. No one could believe that the young singer was really dead.

Selena's funeral was held on April 3, 1995, in Corpus Christi. Television cameras filmed the public funeral, which was broadcast throughout the nation.

Support poured in from around the world. Celebrities like Madonna and Julio Iglesias reached out to Selena's family. Governor George W. Bush declared her birthday "Selena Day" in the state of Texas.

Chris, Suzette, A.B., Abe, and Marcella were heartbroken. Their strong faith in God helped them get through this difficult time.

"I just know that she has eternal life," her father said in an interview.

Selena's final album, *Dreaming of You*, was released on July 18, 1995, less than four months after Selena's death. It contained songs in both English and Spanish, including her ballad to

Chris. Fans hurried to buy the album and hear their favorite singer one final time. The album sold a record-breaking 175,000 copies on the first day. It quickly shot to number one on the music charts. It seemed as if her death had made Selena an even bigger celebrity. For many Americans, *Dreaming of You* was the first time they'd heard of Selena and Tejano music.

Hollywood studio Warner Bros. decided it wanted to make a film about Selena's life. The Quintanillas agreed. They wanted to preserve her legacy and teach new fans about their daughter. Casting the role of Selena would be difficult. They had to find the perfect actress who could capture Selena's spirit. In 1996, it was announced that a young Puerto Rican singer and dancer named Jennifer Lopez would play the role of Selena.

Jennifer Lopez

Her admirers were distressed about the casting choice. Tejano fans thought Selena should be played by a Mexican actress. But the Quintanilla family stood behind the decision to cast Jennifer Lopez in the role. They knew Selena better than anyone, and felt that Lopez was right for the role. Besides, Selena had worked her whole life to bring together different cultures—Anglo and Tejano, Mexican and American. It was important to show that where someone came from didn't define who they were.

Jennifer Lopez actually lived with the Quintanillas to learn more about Selena and get to know her family before filming the movie. On March 21, 1997, *Selena* opened in theaters. Fans rushed to see the screen version of the life story of the incredible Tejano star.

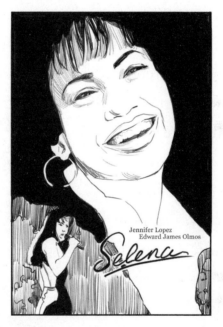

Jennifer Lopez
Edward James Olmos

In the 1990s, Latin American music became more and more popular in the United States and around the world. Singers like Ricky Martin,

Christina Aguilera, Marc Anthony, Enrique Iglesias, and Shakira brought the sounds of Puerto Rico, Ecuador, Colombia, Spain, and other countries to modern American music. Following the release of the movie *Selena*, Jennifer Lopez became an international celebrity. And the decade of the 1990s became known as the "Latin Explosion." Most people believe that Selena helped begin the trend for the entire movement.

Since her death in 1995, Selena's influence has continued to grow. *Dreaming of You* has sold over five million copies. Music historians credit the album with introducing the world to Tejano culture. In 1997, Corpus Christi erected a statue in her honor.

With Suzette's help, a cosmetics company designed a makeup line that perfectly matched Selena's own collection. Fans could wear the same lipstick colors she'd worn on her famous album covers! And in 2017, her status as an international icon was cemented—literally. She was given a star on the famous Hollywood Walk of Fame, alongside so many other superstars.

Although her life was so brief, Selena left a lasting impact on our music, our popular culture, and her own community. Through her confidence, charm, and talent, she brought different cultures, ideas, and people together. Her talent and determination can be heard in her music today, and her legacy continues to inspire fans around the world.

Selena's Influence

Many internationally famous singers credit Selena with influencing their careers.

Beyoncé—"Growing up in Texas, I heard her on the radio. I think listening to her album—even though I didn't know exactly what she was saying—it helped me in the studio with my pronunciation. I think she is a legend. I admire her. She was so talented."

Selena Gomez—"It's such an honor to be named after someone so amazing."

Demi Lovato—"Growing up, I loved Selena's music . . . When I saw the movie, there was just some sort of connection."

Jennifer Lopez—"The impact that she had on my life, on my career . . . It was a great thing for her to be my mentor. And it was a great thing to have her teach me so much about how to navigate this business, but also how to navigate through life."

Selena Gomez, Demi Lovato

Selena Discography

1983	*Selena y los Dinos*	**Freddie Records**
1985	*The New Girl in Town*	**Cara Records**
1986	*Alpha*	**GP Productions**
1987	*And the Winner Is . . .*	**GP Productions**
1989	*Selena*	**EMI Latin**
1990	*Ven Conmigo*	**EMI Latin**
1992	*Entre a Mi Mundo*	**EMI Latin**
1993	*Selena Live!*	**EMI Latin**
1994	*Amor Prohibido*	**EMI Latin**
1995	*Dreaming of You*	**EMI Latin**
1997	*Selena: The Original Motion Picture Soundtrack*	**EMI Latin**
1998	*Selena Anthology* (box set)	**EMI Latin**
2001	*Selena Live! The Last Concert*	**EMI Latin**

2005	*Selena Unforgettable:*	
	The Live Album	**EMI Latin**
	Selena Unforgettable:	
	Ultimate Edition (box set)	**EMI Latin**
2010	*La Leyenda* (box set)	**EMI Latin**

Timeline of Selena's Life

1971 — Selena Quintanilla is born on April 16 in Lake Jackson, Texas

1980 — Papagayos restaurant opens

1982 — The Quintanilla family moves to Corpus Christi, Texas

1983 — Releases her first album, *Selena y Los Dinos*

1985 — Appears on *The Johnny Canales Show*

1986 — Wins Female Vocalist of the Year at the Tejano Music Awards for the first time

1988 — The family gets a tour bus named "Big Bertha"

— Meets Chris Perez while he is playing in the band for Shelly Lares

1990 — Selena receives her high-school diploma

1992 — Marries Chris in secret on April 2

— *Entre a Mi Mundo* is released by Capitol/EMI Latin

1993 — *Selena Live!* is recorded in Corpus Christi

— Selena y Los Dinos sign an English record deal with SBK

1994 — Selena, Etc. store opens in Corpus Christi

— Wins Grammy Award for *Selena Live!*

1995 — Killed on March 31, at age twenty-three

— George W. Bush, then-governor of Texas, declares April 16 "Selena Day" in the state of Texas

Timeline of the World

1971 — Walt Disney World opens near Orlando, Florida

1972 — Shirley Chisholm, the first African American congresswoman, runs for president

— The arcade game *Pong* is released

1974 — Richard Nixon resigns as president of the United States

1976 — The United States celebrates its two hundredth anniversary with a nationwide bicentennial celebration

1980 — The smallpox virus is eradicated

1981 — The first space shuttle, *Columbia*, is launched

1984 — Bruce Springsteen releases *Born in the USA*

1985 — The wreck of the *Titanic* is discovered on the ocean floor

1986 — *The Oprah Winfrey Show* premieres on television

1987 — Michael Jackson releases *Bad*

1989 — The Berlin Wall is demolished in Germany, ending the Cold War

1990 — Nelson Mandela is released from prison after twenty-seven years behind bars

1991 — Operation Desert Storm begins the Persian Gulf War

1993 — *Jurassic Park* comes out in theaters

1995 — America Online provides over one million members with access to the World Wide Web

Bibliography

*Books for young readers

*Marquez, Heron. *Latin Sensations*. Minneapolis: Lerner
Publications, 2001.

Nava, Gregory, director. *Selena*. Los Angeles: Warner Bros., 1997.

Patoski, Joe Nick. *Selena: Como La Flor*. Boston: Little, Brown, 1996.

Peña, Manuel H. *Música Tejana: The Cultural Economy of
Artistic Transformation*. College Station: Texas A&M
University Press, 1999.

Perez, Chris. *To Selena, with Love*. New York: New American
Library, 2012.

San Miguel Jr., Guadalupe. *Tejano Proud: Tex-Mex Music in the
Twentieth Century*. College Station: Texas A&M University
Press, 2002.